Izaak Walton

Izaak Walton

His wallet booke

Izaak Walton

Izaak Walton
His wallet booke

ISBN/EAN: 9783337016043

Printed in Europe, USA, Canada, Australia, Japan

Cover: Foto ©Thomas Meinert / pixelio.de

More available books at **www.hansebooks.com**

Izaak Walton:
HIS
WALLET
BOOKE

CIɔ.Iɔ.CCC.LXXXV.

LONDON:

Field & Tuer, | Sampson Low, Marston.
The Leadenhall Press. | Searle, & Rivington.

Imprynted by
Field & Tuer,
London,
t 4,232.

 RACES & Prefaces cannot be too short: it is therefore merely premised that two centuries have elapsed since "honest old Izaak" was gathered to his fathers, & that this collection of the songs and poesies contained in his "Compleat Angler" is most respectfully dedicated to the wel governed Angler, as well as to the "severe and sowr complexioned."

C.

1885.

Who taught the Lamb
to suck its Mothers
paps?

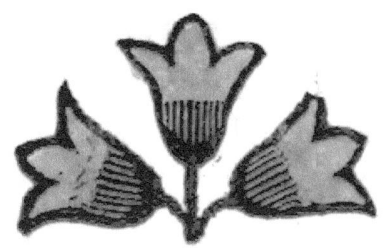

ORD! who hath praise enough? Nay, who hath any?
None can express Thy works, but he that knows them;
And none can know Thy works, they are so many,
And so complete, but only he that owes them.

We all acknowledge both Thy power and love
To be exact, transcendent, and divine;
Who dost so strongly and so sweetly move,
Whilst all things have their end, yet none but Thine.

Wherefore, most sacred Spirit, I here present,
 For me and all my fellows, praise to Thee;
And just it is that I should pay the rent,
 Because the benefit accrues to me.

OD quicken'd in the sea, and in the rivers,
So many fishes of so many features,
That in the waters we may see all creatures,
Even all that on the earth are to be found,
As if the world were in deep waters drown'd.

For seas—as well as skies—have sun, moon, stars;
As well as air—swallows, rooks, and stares;

As well as earth—vines, roses, nettles, melons,
Mushrooms, pinks, gilliflowers, and many millions
Of other plants, more rare, more strange than these,
As very fishes living in the seas;
As also rams, calves, horses, hares and hogs,
Wolves, urchins, lions, elephants, and dogs;
Yea, men and maids; and, which I most admire,
The mitred bishop and the cowlèd friar;
Of which, examples, but a few years since,
Were shown the Norway and Polonian prince.

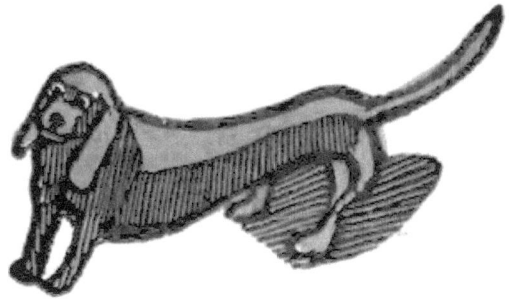

HE adulterous Sargus doth not only change
Wives every day in the deep streams, but, strange!
As if the honey of sea-love delight
Could not suffice his raging appetite,
Goes courting she-goats on the grassy shore,
Horning their husbands that had horns before.

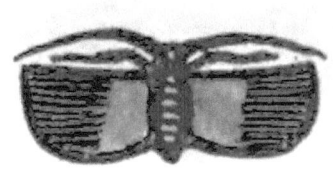

UT contrary, the constant Cantharus
Is ever constant to his faithful spouse;
In nuptial duties spending his chaste life;
Never loves any but his own dear wife.

UT for chaste love the Mullet hath no peer;
For, if the fisher hath surpris'd her pheer, [mate],
As mad with woe, to shore she followeth,
Prest to consort him both in life and death.

HIS day dame Nature seem'd in love;
The lusty sap began to move;
Fresh juice did stir th' embracing vines,
And birds had drawn their valentines.
The jealous trout that low did lie,
Rose at a well-dissembled fly;
There stood my friend with patient skill,
Attending of his trembling quill;
Already were the eaves possess'd
With the swift Pilgrim's daubèd nest;

The groves already did rejoice
In Philomel's triumphing voice;
The showers were short, the weather mild,
The morning fresh, the evening smiled.

   Joan takes her neat-rubbed pail, and now
She trips to milk the sand-red cow;
Where, for some sturdy foot-ball swain,
Joan strokes a syllabub or twain,
The fields and gardens were beset
With tulips, crocus, violet;
And now, though late, the modest rose
Did more than half a blush disclose.

   Thus all looks gay and full of cheer,
   To welcome the new-livery'd year.

ET me live harmlessly, and near the brink
Of Trent or Avon, have a dwelling-place,
Where I may see my quill or cork down sink
With eager bite of perch, or bleak, or dace ;
And on the world and my Creator think :
Whilst some men strive ill-gotten goods t' embrace ;
And others spend their time in base excess
Of wine, or worse, in war and wantonness.

Let them that list, these pastimes still
  pursue,
  And on such pleasing fancies feed their
    fill,
So I the fields and meadows green may
  view,
  And daily by fresh rivers walk at will,
Among the daisies and the violets blue,
  Red hyacinth, and yellow daffodil,
Purple Narcissus like the morning rays,
Pale gander-grass, and azure culverkeys.

I count it higher pleasure to behold
  The stately compass of the lofty sky,
And in the midst thereof, like burning gold,
  The flaming chariot of the world's great
    eye;
The watery clouds that, in the air uproll'd,
  With sundry kinds of painted colours fly;
And fair Aurora lifting up her head,
Still blushing, rise from old Tithonus' bed.

The hills and mountains raisèd from the
    plains,
  The plains extended level with the
      ground ;
The grounds divided into sundry veins,
  The veins enclos'd with rivers running
      round ;
These rivers making way through Nature's
    chains
  With headlong course into the sea
      profound ;
The raging sea, beneath the valleys low,
Where lakes, and rills, and rivulets, do flow.

The lofty woods, the forests wide and long,
  Adorn'd with leaves and branches fresh
      and green,
In whose cool bowers the birds, with many
    a song,
  Do welcome with their choir the Sum-
      mer's Queen ;

The meadows fair, where Flora's gifts among
  Are intermix'd, with verdant grass between ;
The silver-scalèd fish that softly swim
Within the sweet brook's crystal watery stream.

All these, and many more of His creation
  That made the heavens, the Angler oft doth see ;
Taking therein no little delectation,
  To think how strange, how wonderful they be !
Framing thereof an inward contemplation,
  To set his heart from other fancies free ;
And whilst he looks on these with joyful eye,
  His mind is wrapt above the starry sky.

Yn   Yt
Heauen   knowe
schal   and
dwell   doe
Alle   GODS
Crysten   byddyns
Men,   X.

Many a one
Owes to his country his religion;
And in another would as strongly grow,
Had but his nurse or mother taught him so.

 "WAS for that time lifted above earth,

And possess'd joys not promised in my birth."

The Milkmaid's Song.

OME, live with me, and be my love,
And we will all the pleasures prove
That valleys, groves, or hills, or field,
Or woods and steepy mountains yield.

Where we will sit upon the rocks,
And see the shepherds feed our flocks
By shallow rivers, to whose falls
Melodious birds sing madrigals.

And I will make thee beds of roses,
And then a thousand fragrant posies,
A cap of flowers, and a kirtle
Embroider'd all with leaves of myrtle;

A gown made of the finest wool
Which from our pretty lambs we pull;
Slippers lin'd choicely for the cold,
With buckles of the purest gold;

A belt of straw, and ivy-buds,
With coral clasps and amber studs:
And if these pleasures may thee move,
Come, live with me, and be my love.

Thy silver dishes for thy meat,
As precious as the Gods do eat,
Shall on an ivory table be
Prepar'd each day for thee and me.

The shepherd swains shall dance and sing,
For thy delight each May morning :
If these delights thy mind may move,
Then live with me, and be my love.

The Milkmaid's Mother's Answer.

F all the world and love were young,
And truth in every Shepherd's tongue,
These pretty pleasures might me move
To live with thee, and be thy love.

But time drives flocks from field to fold,
When rivers rage and rocks grow cold ;
Then Philomel becometh dumb,
And age complains of care to come.

The flowers do fade, and wanton fields
To wayward Winter reckoning yields.
A honey tongue, a heart of gall,
Is fancy's spring, but sorrow's fall.

Thy gowns, thy shoes, thy beds of roses,
Thy cap, thy kirtle, and thy posies,
Soon break, soon wither, soon forgotten ;
In folly ripe, in reason rotten.

Thy belt of straw and ivy-buds,
Thy coral clasps and amber studs,
All these in me no means can move
To come to thee, and be thy love.

What should we talk of dainties then,
Of better meat than's fit for men?
These are but vain: that's only good
Which God hath bless'd, and sent for food.

But could youth last, and love still breed—
Had joys no date, nor age no need—
Then those delights my mind might move
To live with thee, and be thy love.

MARRIED a wife of late,
The more's my unhappy fate;
I married her for love,
As my fancy did me move,
And not for a worldly estate.

But, oh! the green sickness
Soon changed her likeness,
And all her beauty did fail.
But 'tis not so,
With those that go,
Through frost and snow,
As all men know,
And carry the milking-pail.

Coridon's Song.

H! the sweet contentment
The countryman doth find!
Heigh trolollie lollie loe,
Heigh trolollie lee.
That quiet contemplation
Possesseth all my mind;
Then care away,
And wend along with me.

For Courts are full of flattery,
As hath too oft been tried;
    Heigh trolollie lollie loe, &c.
The City full of wantonness,
And both are full of pride:
    Then care away, &c.

But Oh! the honest countryman
Speaks truly from his heart;
    Heigh trolollie lollie loe, &c.
His pride is in his tillage,
His horses and his cart:
    Then care away, &c.

Our clothing is good sheep-skins,
Grey russet for our wives;
    Heigh trolollie lollie loe, &c.
'Tis warmth, and not gay clothing,
That doth prolong our lives:
    Then care away, &c.

The Ploughman, though he labour
  hard,
Yet on the holiday,
    Heigh trolollie lollie loe, &c.
No Emperor so merrily
Does pass his time away :
    Then care away, &c.

To recompense our tillage,
The Heavens afford us showers ;
    Heigh trolollie lollie loe, &c.
And for our sweet refreshments
The earth affords us bowers:
    Then care away, &c.

The cuckoo and the nightingale
Full merrily do sing,
    Heigh trolollie lollie loe, &c.
And with their pleasant roundelayes
Bid welcome to the Spring :
    Then care away, &c.

This is not half the happiness
The Countryman enjoys;
    Heigh trolollie lollie loe, &c
Though others think they have as much,
Yet he that says so lies;
    Then come away, turn
    Countryman with me.

Jo. CHALKHILL.

The Angler's Song.

AS inward love breeds out-
ward talk,
The hound some praise,
and some the hawk;
Some, better pleas'd
with private sport,
Use tennis; some a mistress court;
But these delights I neither wish,
Nor envy, while I freely fish.

Who hunts, doth oft in danger ride;
Who hawks, lures oft both far and wide;
Who uses games shall often prove
A loser; but who falls in love
  Is fetter'd in fond Cupid's snare:
  My Angle breeds me no such care.

Of recreation there is none
So free as Fishing is alone;
All other pastimes do no less
Than mind and body both possess;
  My hand alone my work can do,
  So I can fish and study too.

I care not, I, to fish in seas—
Fresh rivers best my mind do please,
Whose sweet calm course I contemplate,
And seek in life to imitate:
  In civil bounds I fain would keep,
  And for my past offences weep.

And when the timorous Trout I wait
To take, and he devours my bait,
How poor a thing sometimes I find
Will captivate a greedy mind;
    And when none bite, I praise the wise,
    Whom vain allurements ne'er surprise.

But yet, though while I fish I fast,
I make good fortune my repast;
And thereunto my friend invite,
In whom I more than that delight:
    Who is more welcome to my dish,
    Than to my Angle was my fish.

As well content no prize to take,
As use of taken prize to make:
For so our Lord was pleasèd when
He fishers made fishèrs of men:
    Where (which is in no other game)
    A man may fish and praise his name.

The first men that our Saviour dear
Did choose to wait upon Him here,
Blest fishers were, and fish the last
Food was that He on earth did taste:
  I therefore strive to follow those,
  Whom He to follow Him hath chose.

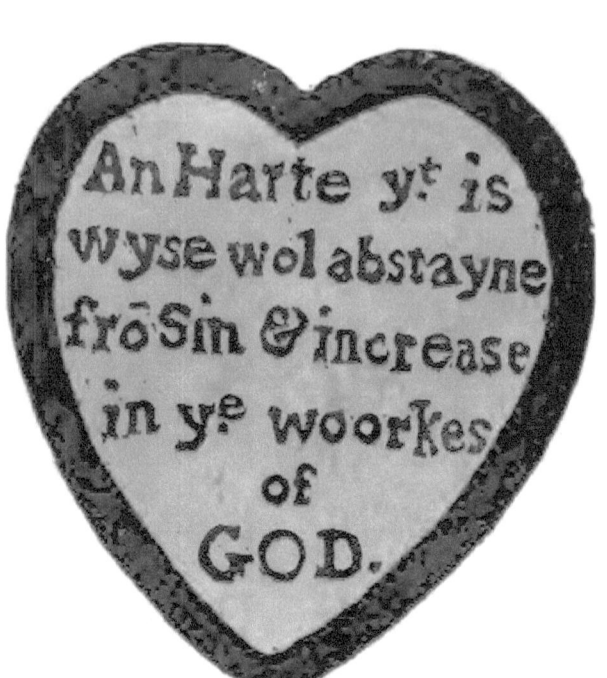

OD, not contented to each kind to give,
And to infuse the virtue generative,
By His wise power made many creatures breed
Of lifeless bodies, without Venus' deed.

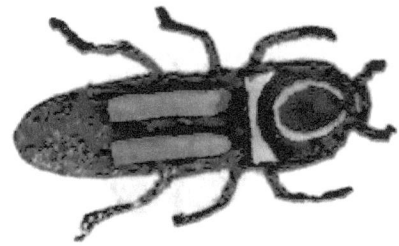

So the cold humour breeds the Salamander,
Who, in effect, like to her birth's commander,
With child with hundred winters, with her touch
Quencheth the fire, though glowing ne'er so much.

So in the fire, in burning furnace, springs
The fly Perausta, with the flaming wings;
Without the the fire it dies; in it it joys;
Living in that which all things else destroys.

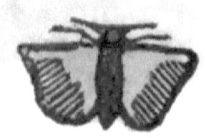

So slow Boötes underneath him sees,
In th' icy islands, goslings hatch'd of trees,
Whose fruitful leaves, falling into the water,
Are turn'd, 'tis known, to living fowls soon after.

So rotten planks of broken ships do change
To barnacles. O transformation strange!
'Twas first a green tree, then a broken hull,
Lately a mushroom, now a flying gull.

When the wind is South,
It blows your bait into a fish's mouth.

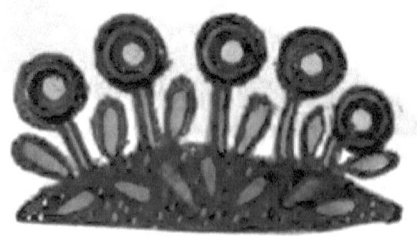

WEET Day, so cool, so
  calm, so bright,
The bridal of the earth
  and sky,
Sweet dews shall weep
  thy fall to-night—
    For thou must die!

Sweet Rose, whose hue, angry and brave,
Bids the rash gazer wipe his eye,
Thy root is ever in its grave—
        And thou must die!

Sweet Spring, full of sweet days and roses,
A box where sweets compacted lie;
My music shows you have your closes—
        And all must die!

Only a sweet and virtuous soul,
Like season'd timber, never gives;
But when the whole world turns to coal,
                    Then chiefly lives!

HAT? *Prayer* by the *Book?* and *Common?* Yes! why not?

    The Spirit of Grace
And Supplication,
Is not left free alone
    For time and place,
But manner too: to *read*, or *speak*, by rote,
    Is all alike to him that prays
    In's heart, what with his mouth he says.

They that in private, by themselves alone
>> Do pray, may take
>> What liberty they please,
>> In choosing of the ways
>> Wherein to make
Their soul's most intimate affections known
> To Him that sees in secret, when
> They're most conceal'd from other men.

But he that unto others leads the way
>> In public prayer,
>> Should do it so
>> As all that hear may know
>> They need not fear
To tune their hearts unto his tongue, and say,
> Amen! not doubt they were betray'd
> To blaspheme, when they meant to have pray'd.

Devotion will add life unto the letter ;
    And why should not
    That which authority
    Prescribes, esteemèd be
    Advantage got?
If the prayer be good, the commoner the better ;
    Prayer in the Church's *words*, as well
    As *sense*, of all prayers bears the bell.
                      CH. HARVIE.

The Angler's Wish.

IN these flowery meads would be :
 These crystal streams should solace me ;
 To whose harmonious bubbling noise
I with my Angle would rejoice :
 Sit here, and see the turtle-dove,
 Court his chaste mate to acts of love :

Or, on that bank, feel the west wind
Breathe health and plenty : please my mind,
To see sweet dewdrops kiss these flowers,
And then, wash'd off by April showers ;
   Here, hear my Kenna sing a song ;
   There, see a blackbird feed her young,

Or a leverock build her nest ;
Here, give my weary spirits rest,
And raise my low-pitch'd thoughts above
Earth, or what poor mortals love :
   Thus, free from lawsuits, and the noise
   Of prince's Courts, I would rejoice ;

Or, with my Bryan and a book,
Loiter long days near Shawford brook ;
There sit by him, and eat my meat,
There see the sun both rise and set ;
There bid good morning to next day,
There meditate my time away ;
    And angle on, and beg to have
    A quiet passage to a welcome grave.

RIGHT shines the sun,
  play, Beggars, play,
Here's scraps enough
  to serve to-day.

What noise of viols is
  so sweet,
As when our merry clappers ring?
What mirth doth want when Beggars meet?
  A Beggar's life is for a king:
Eat, drink, and play—sleep when we list,
Go where we will—so stocks be mist.
  Bright shines the sun; play, Beggars,
    play,
  Here's scraps enough to serve to-day.

The world is ours, and ours alone,
    For we alone have world at will :
We purchase not—all is our own,
    Both fields and streets we Beggars fill :
Nor care to get, nor fear to keep,
Did ever break a Beggar's sleep.
    Bright shines the sun ; play, Beggars, play,
    Here's scraps enough to serve to-day.

A hundred herds of black and white
    Upon our gowns securely feed ;
And yet if any dare us bite,
    He dies therefor, as sure as creed.
Thus Beggars lord it as they please,
And only Beggars live at ease.
    Bright shines the sun ; play, Beggars, play,
    Here's scraps enough to serve to-day.

Piscator fuge ne nocens, etc.

ANGLER! wouldst thou be guiltless? then forbear,

For these are sacred fishes that swim here;

Who know their sovereign, and will lick his hand;

Than which none's greater in the world's command:

Nay, more, they've names, and when they callèd are,

Do to their several owners' call repair.

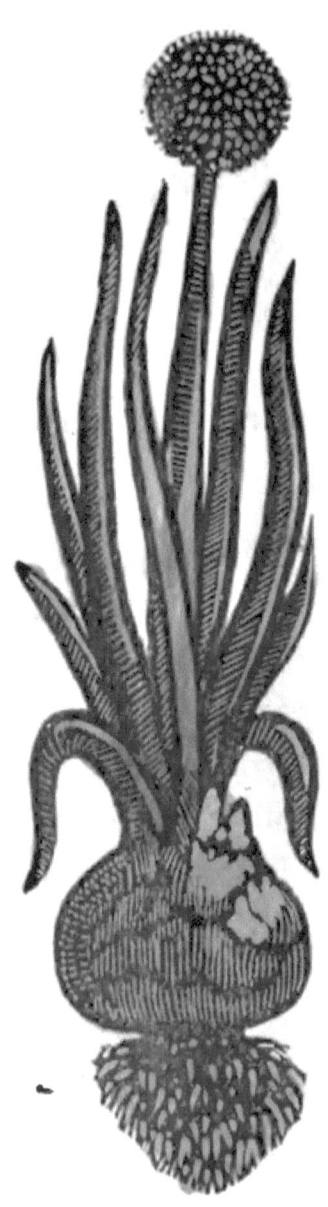

UCIAN, well skilled in scoffing, this hath writ,—
Friend, that's your folly, which you think your wit,
This, you vent oft, void both of wit and fear,
Meaning another, when yourself you jeer.

ND when the Salmon seeks a fresher stream to find,

Which hither from the Sea comes yearly by his kind;

As he tow'rds season grows; and stems the wat'ry tract

Where Tivy falling down, makes a high cataract,

Forc'd by the rising rocks that there her course oppose,

As though within her bounds they meant her to inclose;

Here, when the labouring fish does at the foot arrive,

And finds that by his strength he does but vainly strive;

His tail takes in his mouth, and, bending like a bow

That's to full compass drawn, aloft himself doth throw;

Then springing at his height, as doth a little wand

That, bended end to end, and started from man's hand,

Far off itself doth cast; so does the Salmon vault;

And if at first he fail, his second summersault

He instantly essays; and from his nimble ring,

Still yerking, never leaves until himself he fling

Above the opposing stream.

"OPS and Turkeys, Carps and Beer,

Came into England all in a year."

OME, live with me, and be my love,
And we will some new pleasures prove,
Of golden sands, and crystal brooks,
With silken lines and silver hooks.

There will the river whisp'ring run,
Warm'd by thy eyes more than the sun;
And there th' enamell'd fish will stay,
Begging themselves they may betray.

When thou wilt swim in that live bath,
Each fish, which every channel hath,
Most amorously to thee will swim,
Gladder to catch thee than thou him.

If thou, to be so seen, be'st loth,
By sun or moon, thou dark'nest both;
And if mine eyes have leave to see,
I need not their light, having thee.

Let others freeze with angling-reeds,
And cut their legs with shells and weeds;
Or treach'rously poor fish beset
With strangling snares, or windowy net :

Let coarse bold hands, from slimy nest,
The bedded fish in banks outwrest ;
Let curious traitors sleave silk flies,
To 'witch poor wandering fishes' eyes :

For thee, thou need'st no such deceit,
For thou thyself art thine own bait :
That fish that is not catch'd thereby,
Is wiser far, alas! than I.

H ! the gallant fisher's life,
It is the best of any;
'Tis full of pleasure, void of strife,
And 'tis beloved by many;
Other joys
Are but toys;
Only this
Lawful is;
For our skill
Breeds no ill,
But content and pleasure.

In a morning up we rise,
  Ere Aurora's peeping;
Drink a cup to wash our eyes,
  Leave the sluggard sleeping:
    Then we go
    To and fro,
    With our knacks
    At our backs,
    To such streams
    As the Thames,
  If we have the leisure.

When we please to walk abroad
   For our recreation,
In the fields is our abode,
   Full of delectation :
      Where in a brook
      With a hook,
      Or a lake,
      Fish we take ;
      There we sit
      For a bit,
Till we fish entangle.

We have gentles in a horn,
  We have paste and worms too;
We can watch both night and morn,
  Suffer rain and storms too.
     None do here
     Use to swear;
     Oaths do fray
     Fish away:
     We sit still
     And watch our quill;
Fishers must not wrangle.

If the sun's excessive heat
   Make our bodies swelter,
To an osier hedge we get
   For a friendly shelter;
      Where in a dike,
      Perch or pike,
      Roach or dace,
      We do chase,
      Bleak or gudgeon,
      Without grudging;
We are still contented.

Or we sometimes pass an hour
  Under a green willow,
That defends us from a shower—
  Making earth our pillow:
    Where we may
    Think and pray,
    Before death
    Stops our breath:
    Other joys
    Are but toys,
  And to be lamented.

Jo. Chalkhill.

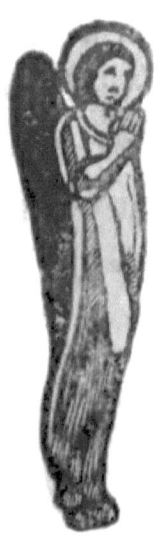

AIL! blest estate of lowliness!
Happy enjoyments of such minds,
As, rich in self-contentedness,
Can, like the reeds in roughest winds,
By yielding make that blow but small,
At which proud oaks and cedars fall.

O empty hopes, no courtly
    fears him fright;
No begging wants his
    middle fortune bite;
But sweet content exiles
    both misery and spite.

His certain life, that never can deceive him,
    Is full of thousand sweets and rich content;
The smooth-leav'd beeches in the field receive him,
    With coolest shade, till noontide's heat be spent :
His life is neither toss'd in boisterous seas,
Or the vexatious world, or lost in slothful ease :
Pleas'd and full bless'd he lives, when he his God can please.

His bed, more safe than soft, yields quiet sleeps,
  While by his side his faithful spouse hath place ;
His little son into his bosom creeps,
  The lively picture of his father's face ;
His humble house or poor state ne'er torment him—
Less he could like, if less his God had lent him ;
And when he dies, green turfs do for a tomb content him.

AN'S life is but vain,
For 'tis subject to pain,
And sorrow, and short as a bubble;
'Tis a hodgepodge of business,
And money, and care;
And care, and money, and trouble.
But we'll take no care
When the weather proves fair:
Nor will we vex
Now though it rain;
We'll banish all sorrow,
And sing till to-morrow,
And angle and angle again.

What is Man?

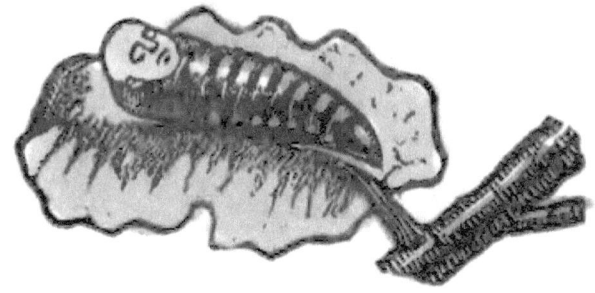

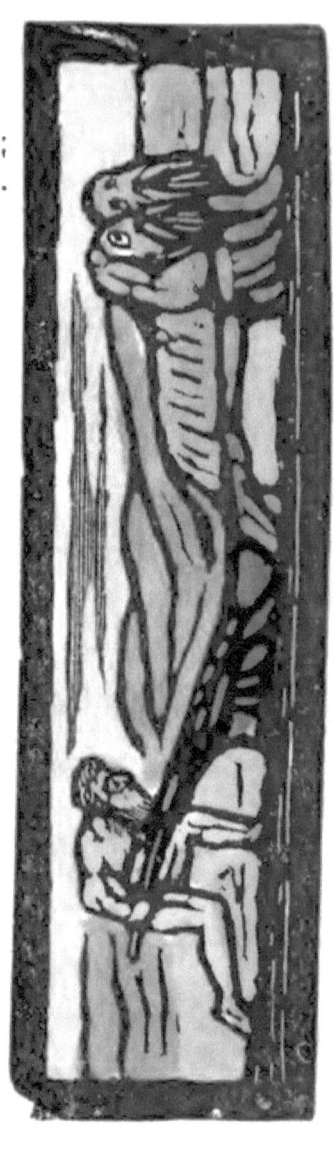

USIC! miraculous rhetoric! that speakest sense
Without a tongue, excelling eloquence;
With what ease might thy errors be excus'd,
Wert thou as truly lov'd as thou'rt abus'd!
But though dull souls neglect, and some reprove thee,
I cannot hate thee, 'cause the angels love thee.

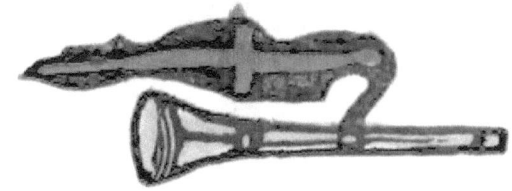

HILST I listen to thy voice,
Chloris, I feel my heart decay:
That powerful noise
Calls my fleeting soul away;
Oh! suppress that magic sound,
Which destroys without a wound!

Peace, Chloris, peace; or singing die,
That together you and I
To heaven may go;
For all we know
Of what the blessèd do above
Is—that they sing and that they love.

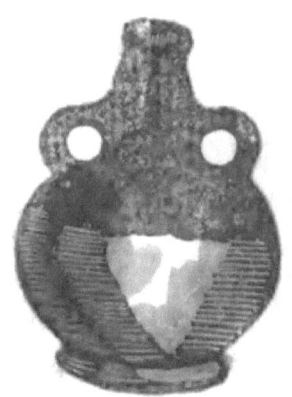

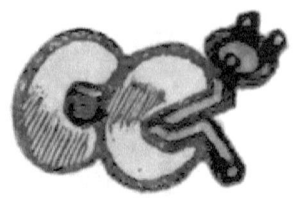

Y rod and my line, my float and my lead,

My hook and my plummet, my whetstone and knife,

My basket, my baits both living and dead,

My net and my meat, for that is the chief:

Then I must have thread, and hairs green and small,

With mine angling-purse—and so you have all.

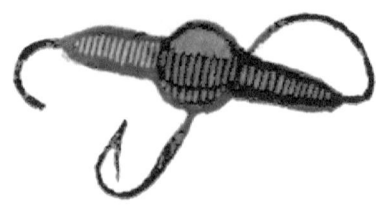

Tot campos, etc.

E saw so many woods and princely bowers,

Sweet fields, brave palaces, and stately towers;

So many gardens dress'd with curious care,

That Thames with royal Tiber may compare.

UR floods' queen, Thames, for ships and swans is crown'd;
And stately Severn for her shore is prais'd;
The crystal Trent, for fords and fish renown'd;
And Avon's fame to Albion's cliffs is rais'd.

Carlegion Chester vaunts her holy Dee;
York many wonders of her Ouse can tell;
The Peak her Dove, whose banks so fertile be,
And Kent will say her Medway doth excel.

Cotswold commends her Isis to the Thame;
  Our northern borders boast of Tweed's fair flood;
Our western parts extol their Willy's fame;
  And the old Lea brags of the Danish blood.

UIVERING fears, heart-tearing cares,
Anxious sighs, untimely tears,
Fly, fly to Courts,
Fly to fond world-lings' sports,
Where strain'd Sardonic smiles are glosing still,
And grief is forc'd to laugh against her will;
Where mirth's but mummery,
And sorrows only real be.

Fly, from our country pastimes, fly,
Sad troops of human misery ;
    Come, serene looks,
    Clear as the crystal brooks,
Or the pure azur'd heaven that smiles to see
The rich attendance on our poverty ;
    Peace and a secure mind,
    Which all men seek, we only find.

Abusèd mortals ! did you know
Where joy, heart's ease, and comforts grow,
    You'd scorn proud towers,
    And seek them in these bowers ;
Where winds, sometimes, our woods perhaps may shake,
But blustering care could never tempest make ;
    Nor murmurs e'er come nigh us,
    Saving of fountains that glide by us.

Here's no fantastic mask nor dance,
But of our kids that frisk and prance;
    Nor wars are seen,
    Unless upon the green
Two harmless lambs are butting one the other—
Which done, both bleating run, each to his mother;
    And wounds are never found,
    Save what the ploughshare gives the ground.

Here are no entrapping baits,
To hasten too, too hasty fates,
    Unless it be
    The fond credulity
Of silly fish, which (worldling-like) still look
Upon the bait, but never on the hook;
    Nor envy, 'less among
    The birds, for prize of their sweet song.

Go, let the diving negro seek
For gems, hid in some forlorn creek :
  We all pearls scorn,
  Save what the dewy morn
Congeals upon each little spire of grass,
Which careless shepherds beat down as they pass;
  And gold ne'er here appears,
  Save what the yellow Ceres bears.

Blest silent groves ! O may you be
For ever mirth's best nursery !
  May pure contents
  For ever pitch their tents
Upon these downs, these meads, these rocks, these mountains,
And peace still slumber by these purling fountains,
  Which we may every year
  Meet, when we come a-fishing here !

AREWELL ye gilded follies, pleasing troubles!

Farewell ye honour'd rags, ye glorious bubbles!

Fame's but a hollow echo—Gold, pure clay—

Honour, the darling but of one short day—

Beauty, th' eye's idol, but a damask'd skin—

State, but a golden prison to live in

And torture free-born minds—Embroider'd trains

Merely but pageants for proud swelling veins—

And blood allied to greatness is alone
Inherited, not purchas'd, nor our own.
> Fame, honour, beauty, state, train, blood, and birth,
> Are but the fading blossoms of the earth.

Izaak

I would be great, but that the sun doth still
Level his rays against the rising hill—
I would be high, but see the proudest oak
Most subject to the rending thunder-stroke—
I would be rich, but see men (too unkind)
Dig in the bowels of the richest mind—
I would be wise, but that I often see
The fox suspected, whilst the ass goes free—

Walton.

I would be fair, but see the fair and proud,
Like the bright sun, oft setting in a cloud—
I would be poor, but know the humble grass
Still trampled on by each unworthy ass—
Rich hated—Wise suspected—Scorn'd if poor—
Great fear'd—Fair tempted—High still envied more :
  I have wish'd all ; but now I wish for neither,
  Great, High, Rich, Wise, nor Fair—Poor I'll be rather.

Would the World now adopt me for her heir—

Would Beauty's queen entitle me the fair—

Fame speak me Fortune's minion—could I vie

Angels with India—with a speaking eye

Command bare heads, bow'd knees, strike justice dumb,

As well as blind and lame; or give a tongue.

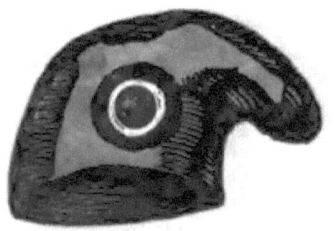

To stones by epitaphs—be call'd "great
  master,"
In the loose rhymes of every poetaster—
Could I be more than any man that lives,
Great, fair, rich, wise, all in superlatives—
Yet I more freely would these gifts resign,
Than ever Fortune would have made them
  mine;
  And hold one minute of this holy leisure,
  Beyond the riches of this empty pleasure!

Welcome, pure thoughts! Welcome, ye silent groves!
These guests, these courts, my soul most dearly loves!
Now the wing'd people of the sky shall sing
My cheerful anthems to the gladsome spring :
A prayer-book now, shall be my looking-glass,
In which I will adore sweet Virtue's face.

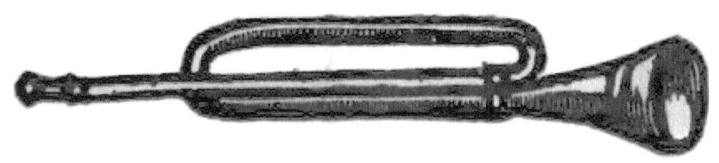

Here dwell no hateful looks, no palace cares,
No broken vows dwell here, nor pale-faced fears;
Then here I'll sit, and sigh my hot love's folly,
And learn t'affect an holy melancholy:
   And if Contentment be a stranger,—then
   I'll ne'er look for it, but in heaven, again.

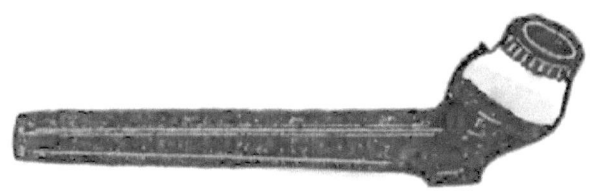

Newly set forth and Adorn'd with

SCVLPTVRES

curiously engraven by

JOSEPH CRAWHALL,

Author of
"The Compleatest Angling Book that ever was writ";
"Border Notes and Mixty-Maxty";
"Chaplets from Coquetside";
"Chap-book Chaplets";
"Olde ffrendes with newe Faces."

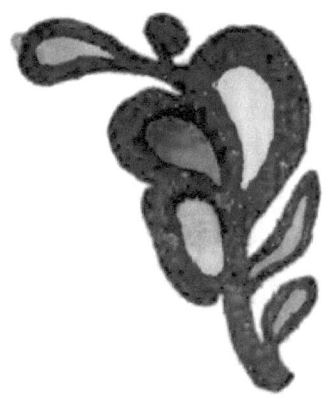

Imprynted at
Yᵉ Leadenhalle Preffe,
50, Leadenhall Street,
London, E.C.

ffield & Tuer

LONDON

Now Ready.] [In One Thick 4to Vol. 25/.

As the many hundreds of illuſtrations are all hand-coloured, the iſſue is neceſſarily limited.

Olde ffrendes
wyth newe Faces.

Adorn'd with futable *SCVLPTVRES*.

TABLE of the matter herein contain'd : I.—The louing Ballad of Lord Bateman. II.—A true relation of the Apparition of Mrs. Veal. III.—The Long Pack: A Northumbrian Tale. IV.—The Sword Dancers. V.—John Cunningham, the Paſtoral Poet. VI.—Ducks & Green Peas, or the Newcaſtle Rider: a Tale in Rhyme. VII.—Ducks and Green Peas: a Farce. VIII.—Andrew Robinſon Stoney Bowes, Eſquire. IX.—The Gloamin' Buchte.

LONDON: Field & Tuer; Simpkin, Marſhall & Co.; Hamilton, Adams & Co.
NEW YORK: Scribner & Welford.

Now Ready.] [In One Thick 4to Vol. 25/.

As the many hundreds of illuſtrations are all hand-coloured, the iſſue is neceſſarily limited.

CRAWHALL'S
Chap-book Chaplets.

Adorn'd with futable *SCVLPTVRES*.

TABLE of the matter herein contain'd : I.—The Barkſhire Lady's Garland. II.—The Babes in the Wood. III.—I Know what I know. IV.—Jemmy & Nancy of Yarmouth. V.—The Taming of a Shrew. VI.—Blew-cap for me. VII.—John & Joan. VIII.—George Barnewel.

LONDON: Field & Tuer; Simpkin, Marſhall & Co.; Hamilton, Adams & Co.
NEW YORK: Scribner & Welford.

Fysshe Stories

Fysshe Stories

Fysshe Stories

Fysshe Stories

Fysshe Stories

Fysshe Stories

Fysshe Stories

Fysshe Stories

Fysshe Stories

Fysshe Stories

Fysshe Stories

Fysshe Stories

Fysshe Stories

Fysshe Stories

Fysshe Stories

Fysshe Stories

Fysshe Stories

Fysshe Stories

Fysshe Stories

Fysshe Stories

Fysshe Stories

Fysshe Stories

Fysshe Stories

Fysshe Stories

Fysshe Stories

Fysshe Stories

Fysshe Stories

Fysshe Stories

Fysshe Stories

Fysshe Stories

Fysshe Stories

Fysshe Stories

Fysshe Stories

Fysshe Stories

Fysshe Stories

Fysshe Stories

Fysshe Stories

Fysshe Stories

Fysshe Stories

Fysshe Stories

Fysshe Stories

Fysshe Stories

Fysshe Stories

Fysshe Stories

Fysshe Stories

Fysshe Stories

Fysshe Stories

Fysshe Stories

Hysshe Stories
I don't believe.

www.ingramcontent.com/pod-product-compliance
Lightning Source LLC
Chambersburg PA
CBHW022115160426
43197CB00009B/1037